Wet Pet

Consultants

Ashley Bishop, Ed.D.
Sue Bishop, M.E.D.

Publishing Credits

Dona Herweck Rice, *Editor-in-Chief*
Robin Erickson, *Production Director*
Lee Aucoin, *Creative Director*
Tim J. Bradley, *Illustrator Manager*
Chad Thompson, *Illustrator*
Sharon Coan, *Project Manager*
Jamey Acosta, *Editor*
Rachelle Cracchiolo, M.A.Ed., *Publisher*

Teacher Created Materials

5301 Oceanus Drive
Huntington Beach, CA 92649-1030
http://www.tcmpub.com

ISBN 978-1-4333-2936-4

© 2012 Teacher Created Materials, Inc.
Printed in Malaysia
THU001.48806

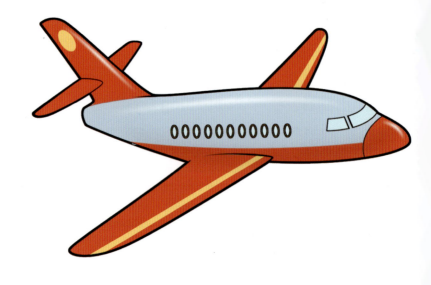

jet

Here is a jet.

wet

The jet is wet.

pet

Here is the pet.

met

I met the pet.

The pet is wet!

Glossary

jet

met

pet

wet

Sight Words

Here is

a   The   I

Extension Activities

Read the story together with your child. Use the discussion questions before, during, and after your reading to deepen your child's understanding of the story and the rime (word family) that is introduced.

The activities provide fun ideas for continuing the conversation about the story and the vocabulary that is introduced. They will help your child make personal connections to the story and use the vocabulary to describe prior experiences.

Discussion Questions
- Why is the jet wet? How does the pet get wet?
- What do cats and dogs do when they get wet?
- Have you ever traveled on an airplane? Would you like to travel on an airplane?

Activities at Home
- Review the *-et* words from the story with your child. Make a list, and add other words that you and your child know, such as *get*, *let*, *net*, *set*, and *yet*. Write a short story together using as many *-et* words as possible.
- Work together with your child to draw different kinds of pets. Talk about your child's work, and encourage him or her to use sight words from the story to talk about the picture: "Here is a pet." "Here is a _____."